To my sunshines Lucy and Ruby.

Winter Gardens

Written by Chelsey Bozarth

Illustrated by Moran Reudor

I wish we could go outside
and plant and play!
But it is very much
       too cold today.

I just want to go outside
and plant some seeds,
because that is exactly
what the garden needs.

Just look outside
and see the cold
snow all around.

We won't be able to plant
them in the frozen ground.

Don't you worry,
there is plenty of room
to prepare for the spring and
the garden's first blooms.

It is exciting
to grow our plants inside.
The love of our home
will keep them alive!

First we have to
find some seeds,

a little bit of potting soil,
and plant feed.

Scoop some soil
in your trays.

Don't worry if you spill,
we will just brush it away

Once our trays are filled to the top,
we will plant our seeds
from our favorite garden shop.

Cover them up with the warm, soft dirt.

Don`t forget to give them
a drink with some water squirts.

Strawberries, tomatoes,
eggplants and many more...
grown from our garden,
they will taste better
than from the store.

Our winter garden
will sprout and thrive.
Tiny baby shoots
will soon arrive.

Turn on the lights and
watch them grow.
It'll be time for spring
before you even know!

Printed in the USA
CPSIA information can be obtained
at www.ICGtesting.com
LVHW081109090224
771186LV00074B/2414

9 798989 470600